A SPECIAL GIFT FOR

_____

from

_____

A LOVING GIFT FOR YOUR CHILDREN

A Mother's *Legacy*

Your Life Story in Your Own Words

THOMAS NELSON
Since 1798

NASHVILLE   DALLAS   MEXICO CITY   RIO DE JANEIRO

Published in Nashville, Tennessee, by Thomas Nelson. Thomas Nelson is a
registered trademark of Thomas Nelson, Inc.

Thomas Nelson, Inc. titles may be purchased in bulk for educational, business,
fund-raising, or sales promotional use. For information, please e-mail
SpecialMarkets@ThomasNelson.com.

ISBN 978-1-4041-1333-6

Designed by Koechel Peterson & Associates, Minneapolis, MN

Printed in Malaysia

Contents

*D*AYS PASS…SEASONS CHANGE…months meld into years, and we stand looking back at our lives—childhood memories, exciting moments, crises, and turning points.

In January we think of new beginnings; in February of valentines, first dates, and first kisses. Does ever a June pass without thoughts of our own wedding day? Surely summer evokes backseat memories of seemingly unending trips to Grandma's house or the beach. And don't November and December bring to mind family traditions and celebrations held tightly through the years?

Introduction

Like ivy on the garden trellis, our lives are inescapably entwined with the seasons and months of the year. That is why we have designed this mother's memory journal in a twelve-month format. Each month features twelve intriguing questions with space to write a personal answer. Questions explore family history, childhood memories, light-hearted incidents, cherished traditions, and the dreams and spiritual adventures encountered in a lifetime of living.

Whether you choose to complete the journal in a few days, weeks, or over the course of a year, the questions will take you on a journey through the times and seasons of your life. This makes a tangible family record to pass on as a gift to a son or daughter, a loving memoir of written words that are windows to a mother's heart.

No matter what your age, memory and reminiscence open a richer, fuller understanding of who you are as a family. Let this memory journal be a starting point—a door into discussing and sharing the unique qualities of your life. May *A Mother's Legacy* draw you closer to each other as you share the experiences of a lifetime.

PERSONAL *Portrait*

YOUR FULL GIVEN NAME

YOUR DATE OF BIRTH

YOUR PLACE OF BIRTH

YOUR MOTHER'S FULL NAME

the place and date of her birth

YOUR FATHER'S FULL NAME

the place and date of his birth

THE NAMES OF YOUR PATERNAL GRANDPARENTS

the places and dates of their births

THE NAMES OF YOUR MATERNAL GRANDPARENTS

the places and dates of their births

THE NAMES OF YOUR SIBLINGS

the places and dates of their births

THE DATE AND PLACE OF YOUR MARRIAGE

THE FULL GIVEN NAME OF YOUR HUSBAND

THE NAMES AND BIRTH DATES OF YOUR CHILDREN

What is your Favorite?

FLOWER _____

PERFUME _____

COLOR _____

HYMN OR SONG _____

BOOK _____

AUTHOR _____

SCRIPTURE, SAYING

OR QUOTATION _____

_____

_____

_____

_____

DESSERT _____

VACATION SPOT _____

TYPE OF FOOD _____

SPORT _____

LEISURE ACTIVITY _____

_____

_____

_____

PERSONAL
PORTRAIT

January

The beauty of the written word

is that it can be held

close to the heart

and read over and over again.

FLORENCE LITTAUER

WHAT WAS YOUR FAVORITE

PASTIME AS A CHILD?

Did you prefer doing it alone

or with someone else?

January

January

WHO GAVE YOU
YOUR NAME AND WHY?
DID YOU HAVE
A FAMILY NICKNAME?
HOW DID YOU GET IT?

14

Describe
your
childhood
bedroom.
What was
the view from
your window?

What was the silliest thing you ever did?

HOW OLD WERE YOU?

What were Sundays like as a child?
Did you go to church?

Visit grandparents?

Was there a family dinner?

If so, what was the typical menu?

WHERE DID YOUR FATHER GO TO WORK EVERY DAY,
and what did he do?

HOW DID YOUR MOTHER SPEND HER DAY?

DID SHE HAVE A JOB OR DO VOLUNTEER

WORK OUTSIDE THE HOME?

January

DESCRIBE WHAT
THE FAMILY LIVING
ROOM LOOKED
LIKE WHEN
YOU WERE A CHILD.

Did you have a favorite bedtime story or a prayer that you said before you went to sleep? Who tucked you in?

Where was your childhood home?

Did you enjoy living there?

DESCRIBE YOUR GRANDPARENTS' HOUSES.

Did you visit them often?
Why or why not?

January

January

LIST ONE SPECIAL

MEMORY

ABOUT EACH

OF YOUR BROTHERS

AND SISTERS.

*Recall for
me some of
the most
important
lessons you
have learned
in life.*

February

For all of us,

today's experiences

are tomorrow's memories.

BARBARA JOHNSON

SHARE A MEMORY OF

YOUR GRANDPARENTS

or an older person you loved:

February

Who have you turned to for advice
or guidance in your life?

AS A YOUNG GIRL, DID YOU PARTICIPATE
IN CHURCH, SCOUTING, OR SOME
OTHER ORGANIZATION OR ACTIVITY?

*How important a role
did that play in your life?*

February

How far did you have to travel to attend
elementary, junior high,
and high school,
and how did you get there?

What scent or sound immediately
*   takes you back to childhood?*

Describe the feeling it evokes.

February

WHAT WAS YOUR
FAVORITE MEAL WHEN
YOU WERE A CHILD?
WHAT MADE IT
YOUR FAVORITE?

*What was
the name
of your
favorite
pet?
Why was
it your
favorite?*

What chores did you have to do when you were
growing up? Which ones did you dislike
most? Which did you not mind doing?

Did you get an allowance?
How much was it?

TELL ME ABOUT YOUR FIRST JOB.

February

SHARE YOUR FAVORITE DESSERT RECIPE:

SHARE A "BAD WEATHER" STORY—
getting caught in a hailstorm,
living without power,
being housebound for days
during a big snowfall.

March

The mother's heart

is the child's schoolroom.

HENRY WARD BEECHER

CAN YOU RECALL AN ESPECIALLY

INTERESTING VISITOR TO YOUR HOME?

*What made that person
or the occasion memorable?*

43

March

WHAT DID YOU WANT
TO BE WHEN YOU GREW
UP? HOW OLD WERE
YOU? DID THAT CHANGE
OVER THE YEARS?

What kinds
of things
do you do
to relax
or renew?
Do you have
a special
place you
like to go?

WHO WAS YOUR FAVORITE TEACHER?
Why?

DESCRIBE ONE OF YOUR FAVORITE DRESS-UP OUTFITS

AS A CHILD.

ON WHAT OCCASIONS WOULD YOU WEAR IT?

Did you ever have a special hideaway or playhouse?

What made it special?

WHAT EXTRACURRICULAR ACTIVITIES WERE YOU INVOLVED IN DURING HIGH SCHOOL?

Why did you choose those activities?

March

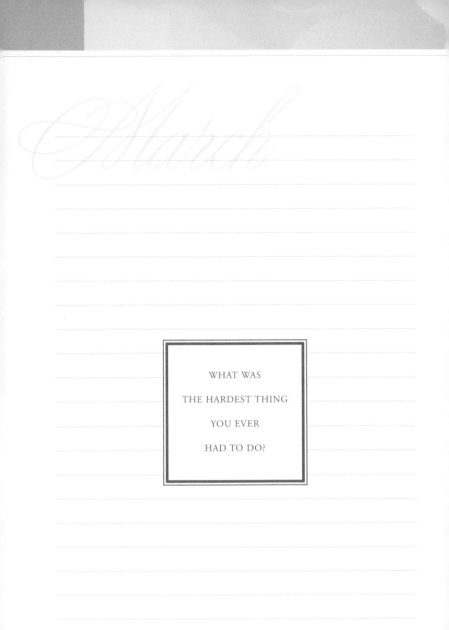

March

WHAT WAS

THE HARDEST THING

YOU EVER

HAD TO DO?

What crazy fads do you remember in grade school?

When did you have your first date? Tell me about it.

WHAT DO YOU REMEMBER ABOUT YOUR FIRST KISS?

What did you do to celebrate birthdays
when you were growing up?

Record here some gardening or decorating tips
that you have found helpful:

April

However time or circumstance

may come between a mother

and her child,

their lives are interwoven forever.

PAM BROWN

WHAT WERE SOME OF THE MOST

MEMORABLE BOOKS

YOU READ AS A CHILD?

What made them memorable?

What were your family finances like
when you were growing up?

How did that affect you?

TELL ABOUT AN AWARD OR HONOR
OR SPECIAL RECOGNITION
YOU HAVE RECEIVED.

April

As a teenager did you rebel
or do things your parents
wouldn't have approved of?

How do you feel about that now?

When did you first learn about sex?

What was your reaction?

WHAT THINGS DO YOU WISH
        YOU HAD DONE IN CHILDHOOD
        OR ADOLESCENCE?

WHAT ARE THE THINGS
YOU ARE MOST GLAD YOU TRIED?

What did your family like to do on weekends?

Describe one particularly memorable event.

HARE ONE OF YOUR MOTHER'S BEST RECIPES

*or a recipe for one of your
favorite childhood dishes.*

April

May

In search of my mother's garden,

I found my own.

WHAT TOYS DID YOU LIKE TO PLAY WITH?

Why those particular toys?

*What is one of the most difficult choices
you ever had to make?*

_____

_____

_____

_____

_____

_____

_____

_____

_____

_____

_____

_____

_____

_____

_____

_____

Would you make the same choice again?

_____

_____

_____

DO YOU REMEMBER A TIME WHEN YOU FELT PARTICULARLY UNSURE OR CONFUSED?

What did you do?

May

DID YOU

EVER GO TO

A DANCE?

TELL ME ABOUT IT.

*What
kind of car
did your
family drive?
Were you
proud of
it or
embarrassed
by it?
Why?*

Did you attend family reunions?

Share a memory of one.

Did you go to church or community potlucks?

How were they important to you and your family?

Tell about someone
      who influenced your life profoundly.

TELL ME ABOUT YOUR BEST
CHILDHOOD FRIEND.

Where did you meet?

What secrets did you share?

What did you like to do?

May

IF YOU WENT TO
COLLEGE OR TO A
CAREER TRAINING
SCHOOL, WHERE DID
YOU GO AND WHY?

Where did
you live
when you
were going
to college or
developing
a career?
Describe an
unforgettable
experience
from that
time in
your life.

WHAT WERE YOUR YOUTHFUL GOALS
AND AMBITIONS FOR LIFE?
Which ones have you been able to fulfill?

ARE THERE CERTAIN SCRIPTURES OR OTHER WRITINGS

THAT YOU REPEATEDLY TURN TO FOR

INSPIRATION OR GUIDANCE?

June

Rings and jewels are not gifts,

but apologies for gifts.

The only gift

is a portion of thyself.

RALPH WALDO EMERSON

IF YOU LEARNED TO PLAY

A MUSICAL INSTRUMENT,

TELL ME YOUR MEMORIES

OF LESSONS, PRACTICE,

AND YOUR MUSIC TEACHER.

If not, what instrument

did you want to play and why?

June

WHAT FASHIONS WERE

POPULAR WHEN YOU

WERE IN HIGH SCHOOL?

DID YOU LIKE THEM?

WHY OR WHY NOT?

*How old
were you
when you
met Dad,
and what
attracted
you
to him?*

When did you first know you wanted to marry him?

What made you feel that way?

SHARE A MEMORY ABOUT THE WAY
HE PROPOSED TO YOU.

June

June

WHAT DID
YOU WEAR
ON YOUR
WEDDING DAY?

*Tell me
about your
wedding
day, from
beginning
to end.*

DID YOUR WEDDING CEREMONY
include a special vow to each other?

What was the significance of it?

Where did you go on your honeymoon?

Share one humorous incident.

What was your first house or apartment together like?

DO YOU REMEMBER ONE
                OF THE MEALS YOU FIXED
        AFTER YOU WERE MARRIED?
        How has your cooking changed since then?

June

WHAT DO YOU LOVE BEST ABOUT DAD NOW?

RECORD HERE SOME TRAVEL TIPS OR SUGGESTIONS

FOR A FUN-FILLED VACATION:

July

look back and see

how I've become who I am

by a family that found

sweetness and joy somewhere inside when . . .

life experience tasted bitter.

KATHY BOICE

SHARE A FAMILY TRADITION

OR MEMORY

FROM THE FOURTH OF JULY.

Have you ever participated in a rally
or demonstration?

What was the cause?

Why did you participate?

WHO IN YOUR FAMILY SERVED
IN THE MILITARY AND WHEN?

Do you have a special memory of that person?

July

DID YOU LEARN

TO SWIM?

HOW?

*Did you
take family
vacations?
Record one
especially
memorable
experience.*

Tell about your first trip by plane, train, or ship.

How old were you?

Were you excited? Nervous?

IF YOU EVER TRAVELED ABROAD, WHAT WAS THE
MOST UNIQUE EXPERIENCE OF THE TRIP?

*If you haven't been abroad, what foreign
country would you most like to visit? Why?
Did you visit them often? Why or why not?*

July

109

DESCRIBE THE MOST FASCINATING PLACE YOU HAVE VISITED.

TELL ABOUT A DRIVING TRIP WITH YOUR FAMILY.

*Did your relatives come to visit
in the summer or did you go to visit them?*

What are your memories of those visits?

HOW DID YOU LEARN TO DRIVE?

What was your first car like?

DID A TRAGEDY

EVER STRIKE

YOUR FAMILY?

HOW WERE

YOU AFFECTED?

Share a favorite poem or a passage of writing that has been especially meaningful in your life.

August

The family—

that dear octopus from whose tentacles

we never quite escape,

nor, in our inmost hearts, ever quite wish to.

DODIE SMITH

NAME A BOOK OR AUTHOR

THAT HELPED YOU DEVELOP

A PHILOSOPHY OF LIFE.

Share some of those insights.

August

119

Did you have a collection when you were growing up?

*What initially sparked
your interest in it?*

DESCRIBE A PERFECT SUMMER DAY.

August

August

WHAT KIND OF

OUTDOOR WORK

DO YOU LIKE?

HATE? WHY?

If you could be a patron of a charity or organization, which one would you choose? Why?

When did you learn how to ride a bike,

OR TO WATER SKI, SNOW SKI, ROLLER SKATE, OR SAIL?

Share your memories of the experience.

What summer games and activities did your family enjoy?

Did you ever milk a cow
or spend time on a farm or in the country?

Tell me about it.

DESCRIBE YOUR FIRST TRIP ALONE.

August

August

WHAT PLACES
WOULD YOU STILL
LIKE TO VISIT?
WHY?

Describe a frightening or difficult experience from childhood. How did you respond to it?

TELL ME ABOUT YOUR MOST
UNFORGETTABLE SUMMER
EXPERIENCE AS A CHILD.

SHARE SOME OF YOUR IDEAS

ABOUT SUCCESSFUL ENTERTAINING.

September

Our lives are a mosaic of little things,

like putting a rose

in a vase on the table.

INGRID TROBISCH

DID YOU LEARN TO SEW

OR MAKE OTHER CRAFTS?

How and when?

What was the first thing you made?

What were your favorite subjects in grade school?

junior high?

high school?

What was your major in college?

Would you choose that major again? Why or why not?

AS A YOUNG PERSON DID YOU VOLUNTEER

for work in church, community,
or social services?

Tell me about your experiences.

When did you move away from home?

Describe where you lived
        and how you felt about it.

WHO WAS YOUR BEST FRIEND AFTER YOU WERE MARRIED?

Describe some of the fun things
you did together. Are you still friends?

September

September

WHAT IS SOMETHING

YOU LEARNED

FROM AN ESPECIALLY

DIFFICULT TIME

IN YOUR LIFE?

*What is
something
you learned
from an
especially
happy
time
in your
life?*

WHAT SPECIAL TALENTS DID YOUR PARENTS NURTURE IN YOU?

How have you developed those talents?

What would you like to learn to do?

Why?

September

WHAT WOULD

YOU DO

DIFFERENTLY

IN LIFE

IF YOU COULD?

Describe your personal style in clothing, makeup, skin care, hair care.

October

How will our children know who they are

if they don't know

where they came from?

MA IN GRAPES OF WRATH

WHO ARE SOME OF

THE BEST SPEAKERS

YOU HAVE EVER HEARD?

Why?

October

HOW WOULD YOU

LIKE TO BE

REMEMBERED?

WHY IS THIS

IMPORTANT TO YOU?

What are some of the things that make you smile when you think of them?

WHAT DO YOU CONSIDER
to be some of life's most difficult challenges?

WHAT DO YOU CONSIDER TO BE LIFE'S GREATEST GIFTS?

What responsibilities did your parents require of you as a child?

EXPLAIN HOW THIS AFFECTED YOUR GROWTH AND DEVELOPMENT.

NAME YOUR FAVORITE HOBBY.
WHEN AND WHERE
DID YOU START DOING IT?

Why do you enjoy it?

October

When and where did you buy your first house?

*Describe the house and explain
any significance it held for you.*

WHAT IS THE STRANGEST THING
YOU HAVE EVER SEEN?

Tell about a memorable hotel
or resort you have visited. Describe the location
AND TELL ABOUT EXPERIENCES THAT WERE SIGNIFICANT.

DID YOU EVER GO ON A HAYRIDE OR BOB FOR APPLES?

What other fun activities did you
and your friends or classmates enjoy?

October

*As a teenager, did you belong
to a club or church youth group?*

*Tell me about the individuals
in the group who were
most significant to you.*

SHARE SOME HELPFUL HOME REMEDIES

or tips for good health.

November

In our family an experience was not finished,

nor truly experienced,

unless written down

or shared with another.

ANNE MORROW LINDBERGH

WHAT INDIVIDUALS HAVE HAD

THE GREATEST IMPACT

ON YOUR LIFE?

In what way?

November

November

WHAT IS YOUR

MOST TREASURED

POSSESSION

AND WHY?

*Who were
your female
role models
when you
were growing
up? How
have they
affected the
kind of person
you are?*

WHAT IS YOUR MOST VIVID MEMORY
OF BEING PREGNANT?

HOW DID YOU CHOOSE MY NAME AND WHY?

WHAT IS YOUR MOST POIGNANT MEMORY ABOUT MY CHILDHOOD?

What was a favorite
Thanksgiving tradition
in your family?

November

WHAT ARE SOME

THINGS FROM

YOUR CHILDHOOD

THAT YOU ARE

THANKFUL FOR?

What childhood memory first comes to mind when you think about winter? How do you respond to that memory?

What are some of the things you remember most from your childhood

EXPERIENCES AT CHURCH OR SCHOOL

OR IN YOUR NEIGHBORHOOD?

Do certain people come to mind?

What family custom would you like to pass on
to your children and grandchildren?

November

WHAT NEW TRADITION
WOULD YOU LIKE TO
START IN THE FAMILY?
WHAT IS ITS
SIGNIFICANCE?

*Share a
favorite
Thanksgiving
or Christmas
recipe.*

December

If everything special and warm and happy

in my formative years

could have been consolidated

into one word,

that word would have been Christmas.

GLORIA GAITHER

TELL ABOUT

SOME CHRISTMAS RITUALS

IN YOUR FAMILY

and how you felt about them.

December

December

WERE YOU EVER IN A

CHRISTMAS PROGRAM?

HOW DID YOU

RESPOND TO

THE EXPERIENCE?

What favorite Christmas treasures have you kept from year to year? Share their origins.

Tell about a memorable
        Christmas visit with relatives.

WHAT IS YOUR FAVORITE CHRISTMAS CAROL?

Why?

*Did you have a Christmas stocking
as a child or a special ornament?*

What did it look like?

DESCRIBE THE CHRISTMAS

that has been the most meaningful to you.

December

WHAT WOULD BE

THE MOST

WONDERFUL GIFT

YOU COULD RECEIVE?

WHY?

What have people older than you taught you about life? What have you learned from children and young people?

WHAT WOULD YOU LIKE TO SEE HAPPEN
in the next ten years?

WHAT WAS ONE OF THE BEST SURPRISES YOU EVER HAD?

A PARTY? A GIFT? AN UNEXPECTED FAVOR?

DID YOU EVER SURPRISE SOMEONE ELSE?

IN WHAT WAY?